Scaramouch in Naxos by John Davidson

A PANTOMIME

John Davidson was born at Barrhead, East Renfrewshire on 11th April 1857.

In 1862 his family moved to Greenock and there he began his education at Highlanders' Academy. Davidson would now spend many years at school and the beginnings of a career in various industries before gaining employment in various schools.

By now literature was a large part of his activities and his first published work was 'Bruce, A Chronicle Play' in 1886. Four other plays quickly followed including the somewhat brilliant pantomimic 'Scaramouch in Naxos' (1889).

With his reputation gradually providing an income he was also able to explore his true medium; Verse. 'In a Music Hall and Other Poems' (1891) together with 'Fleet Street Eclogues' (1893) were ample proof that he possessed a quite rare, genuine and distinctive poetic gift.

Davidson now turned further and further towards verse. In 1894 he published his most popular volume, 'Ballads and Songs' (1894), and this was followed by a further 'Fleet Street Eclogues' (Second Series) (1896) and by 'New Ballads' (1897) and 'The Last Ballad' (1899).

As the new century dawned Davidson was hard at work on a series of 'Testaments', in which he gave definite expression to his philosophy and were published over a seven year period; 'The Testament of a Vivisector' (1901), 'The Testament of a Man Forbid' (1901), 'The Testament of an Empire Builder' (1902), and 'The Testament of John Davidson' (1908).

However, on 23rd March 1909, with his finances in ruins, the onset of cancer and profound hopelessness and clinical depression he left his house for the last time. His body was only found on September 18th by some local fishermen.

Index of Contents

I0158431

PERSONS

Bacchus
Silenus
Sarmion
Glaucus
Scaramouch, a Showman
Harlequin, in the employment of Scaramouch
Ariadne
Ione, daughter to Glaucus
Columbine, in the employment of Scaramouch
Satyrs
Bacchantes
Sailors

SCENE: Naxos.

PROLOGUE

SILENUS

Gentle readers—I would fain say, hearers, but I am afraid I shall never fool it on the stage—I am very fond of Pantomimes. I don't know whether I like this one so well as I liked those which I witnessed when I was a boy. It is too pretentious, I think; too anxious to be more than a Pantomime—this play in which I am about to perform. True Pantomime is a good-natured nightmare. Our sense of humour is titillated and strummed, and kicked and oiled, and fustigated and stroked, and exalted and bedevilled, and, on the whole, severely handled by this self-same harmless incubus; and our intellects are scoffed at. The audience, in fact, is, intellectually, a pantaloon, on whom the Harlequin-pantomime has no mercy. It is frivolity whipping its schoolmaster, common-sense; the drama on its apex; art, unsexed, and without a conscience; the reflection of the world in a green, knotted glass. Now, I talked to the author, and showed him that there was a certain absence from his work of this kind of thing; but he put his thumbs in his arm-pits, and replied with some disdain, "Which of the various dramatic forms of the time may one conceive as likeliest to shoot up in the fabulous manner of the beanstalk, bearing on its branches things of earth and heaven undreamt of in philosophy? The sensational dramas? Perhaps from them some new development of tragic art; but Pantomime seems to be of best hope. It contains in crude forms, humour, poetry, and romance. It is the childhood of a new poetical comedy." Then I saw where he was, and said, "God be with you," and washed my hands of him. But I'll do my best with my part.

SCENE I.—A Wood

SILENUS, sitting. **HARLEQUIN** and **COLUMBINE** posturing about him. **SATYRS** and **BACCHANTES** dancing round the group.

Song.

Sing of dancing, sing of wine,
    Satyrs and Bacchantes, sing.
Harlequin and Columbine,
    Leap within our frantic ring.

    Dance, the skies are violet;
        Dance, our lips with wine are wet;
    Sing, heigh-ho, the shade is mellow!
        Twist and twine from dusk till dawn;
    Feet and hoofs beat bare the lawn.
        Bacchus is a noble fellow!

From our garlands grapes are flung,
    And we tread them in the grass;
Ivy, in our tresses strung,
    Streams behind us as we pass.

    Dance, the skies are violet;
        Dance, our lips with foam are wet;
    Sing, the beechen shade is mellow!
        Bend and bound with one accord;
    Foot it firm, and trench the sward.
        Bacchus is a splendid fellow!

Round we spin; our starry eyes
    Glimmer through our tossing manes.
Time is ending; wisdom dies;
    We are drunk; and Bacchus reigns.

    Dance, the skies are violet;
        The dust with juice of grapes is wet;
    Sing, the deepening shade is mellow!
        Dance the night into the day;
    Dance into eternity.
        Bacchus is the only fellow!

HARLEQUIN

Now, you may tell them; now, that they think of Bacchus but as one of themselves—a wine-bibber, and the inventor of wine-bibbing.

SILENUS

Do you disparage wine-bibbing?

HARLEQUIN

May my mask grow to my face, and my sword to my arm, if I do not think it a most intellectual pursuit! Columbine. For what do you take us?

SILENUS

No enigmas: I am not good at riddles in the evening; for the tedious parched hours of this torrid July, and the labour of moistening them make me sweat brains; but if I have not enough left to say what I take you for I would be glad to mount spontaneously to heaven in a chariot of fire—I mean by combustion. You, my good Harlequin, I take to be the son of Mercury and one of the furies.

HARLEQUIN

Which one?

SILENUS

Know you not your own mother? She whom Hermes mistook for Aphrodite: it's an old story now, as your joints might tell you, for you are a most degenerate

HARLEQUIN

Now do I remember Bathylus and Pylades, sweet youths both.

HARLEQUIN

Were they Harlequins?

SILENUS

Harlequins! They were anything. Their very hands were garrulous as beldames, and their fingers more exclamatory than Marsyas under the knife of Apollo. You are a mere grasshopper and a magpie—a very signboard. You are like your father in nothing but the lightness of your heels, and the nimbleness of your pilfering.

HARLEQUIN

In what am I like my mother?

SILENUS

In greed, and in that you are appointed to be my torment. But you serve me, too, or I would discard you. Moreover, you amuse me. You are a walking firmament: your spangles are the milky way, and your belt the zodiac. Sometimes you are Orion, and swagger out with sword on thigh to ogle the Pleiades. You are the bad angel of pleasantry, because you are, as it were, humour run to seed, and become a science: you are a mere name, and the thing which you once were is in limbo; wherefore you suit these times, and are well matched with my sweet Columbine. Columbine. What am I?

SILENUS

What short flounces and limelight have made you. What do these woods know of fleshings? Doff them for shame, and go naked. Columbine.
[Aside]
Swell till you burst, old pumpkin! We'll make a pantaloon of you before we've done.

SILENUS

What are you muttering? Do you hear? You must go naked with a tiger's skin.

HARLEQUIN

She shall. But see, they are ripe for your address.

SILENUS

I say, wine-bibbing is noble, and drunkenness a virtue. Give me a drink, and let me go to sleep.

HARLEQUIN

Have you forgotten?

SILENUS

I thank Jove I have. To forget is Elysium; regret is hell. I would put it better if I weren't so sleepy.

HARLEQUIN

This will rouse you.

[Gives him wine. **SILENUS** drinks.

Aurora is in this wine: already I feel her chariot prancing through my veins. I have drunken of the sun. Children—
[Aside]
What was I to say? There was some plot. Harlequin
[Aside]
You are Bacchus.

SILENUS

I am the new Bacchus—

HARLEQUIN [Aside]

No, no; you are the old Bacchus!

SILENUS

—and the old Bacchus, and Bacchus altogether; and that maiden-faced Bacchus, who these many generations has roamed about the world striking men with fury and madness, is not the son of Semele, but a pampered and audacious old mountain-rover, none other than my ancient, Silenus, disguised. And this is the meaning of the fable that says I was dead and buried for a time. What greater burial could there be than the eclipse of Bacchus by Silenus! Well then, I am Bacchus: Proserpina nursed me.

HARLEQUIN

The true Bacchus is come again! All. Long live the true Bacchus!

SILENUS

There shall be no more rations, but all shall drink as much as they please; for ever since I stepped out of Jove's thigh I have been a hard drinker.
[Aside]
Do I not do it well? Observe how I throw in these back-handers about my parentage—casually—before I am aware; and I blush and hem, for I would not be thought proud.—Children, rumour has confounded me with my father, Jupiter. Think it not: I am plain Bacchus, whose only claims on the world are that he invented wine, and is a good fellow, and a hard drinker. Fear me not, for I am harmless.

ALL

Long live Bacchus!

SILENUS
Columbine, where is Ariadne? Columbine. I do not know, but we must find her.

SILENUS
We must.—I have no chariot.

HARLEQUIN
You shall have one.

SILENUS
And tigers?

HARLEQUIN
I fear you can't have tigers: there are none on the island.

SILENUS
Then you must get me some cats instead. And now I bethink me, cats will please me better. They were dangerous reptiles, those tigers, and I am growing old: my charms have not the power they once had. Harness me some half-dozen tabbies: they shall serve well enough. I have somewhat more to say, and I will say it seriously.
[Rises]
Drinkers and drunkards, gentle profligates, In praise of drinking to be curious Would task Apollo and his morning lyre, With fresh and dulcet brains and strings new-strung, So often has the art been sung and said: And yet good reasons for it scarce are known: One that consoles me I will offer you. We are immortals—all of us, divine; But people of inferior intellect. Wherein consists our chief capacity? In drinking deep: and some have sprightly toes. Well, here's my reason. What is genius? This: Perception of our bent and tireless zeal To track it out against the wind of fate. Have we not followed with a quenchless thirst Deep drinking?

ALL
We have, most noble Bacchus.

SILENUS
Are we not plagued with headaches in the morning?

ALL
We are, we are.

SILENUS
Some of our noses, too, are rubicund.

ALL
Most true.

SILENUS
Our eyes are bulging, blazing amethysts.

1st SATYR
Grapes, bursting grapes.

SILENUS
The women's hair is dank as Panope's, Uncrisped and colourless, as limp as hay.

BACCHANTES
Alas! alas!

SILENUS
Their cheeks are hollow, and their arms are thin.

BACCHANTES
Alack-a-day!

SILENUS
We all are rebels.

1st SATYR
Outcasts

1st BACCHANTE
Unsexed.

2nd BACCHANTE
Lost.

SILENUS
Then are we geniuses. Now, hear my reason.

1st SATYR
Your reason!

2nd SATYR
Why, we thought we had it now!

SILENUS
Erroneous conclusion; for to say That we have geniuses for drinking deep, And drink accordingly, is but to say We drink because we're dry: that's not enough. Reason there is for genius evermore, Could we discover it.

1st SATYR
Then tell us ours.

SILENUS
Patience and drink a little.

[**ALL** drink.

Mine alderliefest prodigals, the truth Is simply this, that we're inferior.

1st BACCHANTE
We know it.

SILENUS
Well said! That's it! We know it! Inferior, and we know it. Consider, then, What dreadful thought is this—what dire dismay—Inferior, yet immortal! We tried, we failed; Failure was our familiar: so we chose, Rather than miss our aim eternally, To aim to miss, making success secure: That is the reason of our geniuses. Were we of those to whom death ministers, We might strain struggling, staggering—but no! What is the highest life that mortals live? A finger-length—time, fame, oblivion— A slate, a pencil, and a sponge! Then drink.

Song and dance, in which SILENUS joins.

 Dance and sing, we are eternal;
  Let us still be mad with drinking:
 'Tis a madness less infernal
  Than the madness caused by thinking.

 Death, cease whetting missiles for us;
  Lurk not in the grave's dark portal;
 Bring your dead, and join the chorus;
  Drink, for we are all immortal.

 Drink, my gallants; reel and rhyme
  Though our souls are second-rate
 We are none the less sublime:
  Drink, and give the lie to fate!

SILENUS
I know another song like that; but if drunkenness is no excuse for plagiarism, what is?

[**SILENUS**, **SATYRS**, and **BACCHANTES** go out.

[Enter **SCARAMOUCH**.

HARLEQUIN
Welcome, great chief! Columbine. Hail, noble champion!

SCARAMOUCH
How d'ye do? How d'ye do? Have you secured our venerable Bacchanalian friend?

HARLEQUIN
We have.

SCARAMOUCH

Where is he? Now, don't tell me he's in your pocket. I'm not yet better of that fairy you caught me.

HARLEQUIN

Was she not a success?

SCARAMOUCH

O Harlequin! O Columbine! I had her advertised on posters as big as mainsails. I paid municipalities fortunes to permit policemen to be my sandwich-men.

HARLEQUIN

And a very good use to put them to.

SCARAMOUCH

Now don't: I can't stand it. Listen: I offered a prize of a thousand guineas to whoever would make a new joke about policemen, introducing my fairy. Twenty-one thousand jokes were sent in: I read these jokes.

HARLEQUIN

Heroic soul!

SCARAMOUCH

Nay, I am better. Do not flatter me.—Well, I published an hourly bulletin of the fairy's progress to the capital, with gratis supplements of original novels by the chief living writers. I hired and shut up six theatres, and bought the Crystal Palace to exhibit her in. Age of glass and iron! there came a thing about the size of a small tadpole!

HARLEQUIN

Well, I never said she was a giantess.

SCARAMOUCH

No; but my bills had her as big as a ballet-girl. The crowd—there was a crowd the first and only night—couldn't see it; so they wrecked the Palace and went off in a body to the performing fleas, and a stray cat ate the fairy. Now, how big is Bacchus?

HARLEQUIN

Too big for a cat to eat: in fact, I don't believe any cat in Christendom, even Whittington's, which bearded a king, would dare to look at him. I only saw him once, and I've no desire to see him again. He withered me, sir, with a look: I am limp still.

SCARAMOUCH

Paper, pens, and ink! I thought you said you had him?

HARLEQUIN

No, sir; we have only got his venerable Bacchanalian friend.

SCARAMOUCH

People and pantomimes! what am I to do!

HARLEQUIN

Ship Silenus instead. Why, even supposing we could get hold of Bacchus, he would be of no use for our purpose. Columbine. He would be a worse bargain than the fairy, unless you passed him off for Ariadne.

SCARAMOUCH

In the name of the living tinker, how?

HARLEQUIN

Because not a soul would believe that the big beardless boy which Bacchus looks was he. Now, this old wine-skin, Silenus, is just the idea your worthy patrons have of what Bacchus must be after a supposed debauch extending from end to end of the Christian era.

SCARAMOUCH

And is he willing to play Bacchus?

HARLEQUIN

As willing as a grub is in May to be a butterfly. Bacchus has placed him and some other drouths of his crew under guard, and limited them to so many drinks a day, for they were as dissipated as porters. I helped them to escape on condition that they should sail with us; which was a bargain. But they were more difficult to manage than a crew ashore after a three months' voyage. Imagine, now: they have gone off in search of Ariadne. By good chance they took the way to the beach.

SCARAMOUCH

Is Ariadne in the wood?

HARLEQUIN

Not at all: but they have all shipped such a sea of liquor that they would believe anything. Silenus told them to go and find Ariadne, and they straightway comprehended that she was in the vicinity.

SCARAMOUCH

I suppose we couldn't lay hands on her? Columbine. On Ariadne? you might as well try to lay hands upon a star.

SCARAMOUCH

Stripes and stirrups! a glorious idea! To have a well-preserved planet or a three-tailed comet on exhibition! Naxos and night! but that would be stupendous.

> For a caravan is the only plan;
>   Hurry my toms and trulls!
> Ho-ye-ho, and a rumble-low!
> Pay your penny, and see the show:
>   This is the age of gulls.

[They go out dancing.

SCENE II.—The Sea-shore

Enter **IONE**.

IONE
O wind, and do you wander all the night,
Moving the broad, black clouds, heavy and high,
And lifting, there and yonder, with a kiss,
The wet plumes of the sea? O sweet west wind,
Stay here and tell me secrets for a while!
Whence do you come and whither are you bound?
What music are you singing to yourself,
Sometimes with muffled syllables that fall,
And break their meaning on the hearts they touch?
Is this the wind that turned against her mouth
Forsaken Ariadne's wrathful sighs?
I see her leaning on her clenched right hand,
As she awakes and knows the flying sail,
And thinks that even to her has man been false,
Hatred and scorn—no sorrow, love, nor dread—
Starting in tears from both her angry orbs.—
My foot is wet! The tide is thronging up
With jocund whispers, and the press of waves
Scatters in pearly laughter on the sand.
Surely the moon is arming for the night:
O, now, I see her silver harness gleam
Behind the dusky curtains of her tent!
While the wind, swelling, sounds a trumpet-note,
She showers her bounteous shadow on the sea,
A largesse to the waves that toss their caps:
And now she leaps into the lists of heaven.—
What creature in her shadow floats this way?
It is a boat, and one sits at the helm!

[Hides behind a rock.

The sail is silken, and the hull, pearl-clad;
It leaps from wave to wave: the sweet, salt spray,
Like odoured tresses loosened in the dance,
Streams from the prow. This is some god: he lands.—
If he be man, the men that I have known
Are of a lower order. How the moon
Shines on him! and his eyes drink in her light.
He cannot know our world. Now on the sea,
Now on the shore, he flings his looks about;
And yet again, the moon. What if he be
Endymion! O, would I were the moon!
What! has he seen me?

[**SARMION** enters and leads her from her hiding-place.

Are you man or god?

[He makes a sign.

Can you not speak? Poor mariner, he's dumb!
What shall I do with him? Be not afraid;
No one shall harm you, for my father owns
The land here and the shore. I left our house
Without his knowledge and against his will
That I might see the sea alone at night:
I never felt such ecstasy before:
I will frequent the strand, and with the moon
Keep company. You love the moon, I think?

VOICE [Within]
Ione, Ione!

My father's voice!

[Enter **GLAUCUS**.

GLAUCUS
Well, why don't you introduce me?

IONE
Are you angry?

GLAUCUS
O no! I have run a mile through thorns and bents and sand, but I am not angry. I may be hot and out of breath, and my head may steam like a punch-bowl, but I am not angry. I fell ten or twelve times and harrowed the soil with my countenance, but I am not angry. My daughter, sir—this is my daughter, the sauciest madcap in Naxos—runs out of the house when she should be asleep, to meet you in this unwholesome moonlight, and she asks me if I am angry! Why, sir, a man who could be angry in these circumstances would be a man of an infinitesimal mind. My body may be one bruise; my heart may be broken into cat's meat; but I am not angry: do not think it.

[**IONE** and **GLAUCUS** talk apart.

IONE
This is a god.

GLAUCUS
A what?

IONE
One of the minor gods.

GLAUCUS
I wouldn't have thought it. What's his name?

IONE
I do not know. He slid down a moonbeam in that boat you see, and sailed ashore five minutes ago. He has not spoken yet, nor will he speak. I think he has done something for which Jove is punishing him with dumbness.

GLAUCUS
Poor fellow! I'd sooner be blind.

IONE
I believe you, father. I think you should ask him to the house.

GLAUCUS
Do you? Are they not rather ticklish customers, these gods?

IONE
No; they are charming company.

GLAUCUS
Oh!—But this is an anonymous god. People would laugh at us, and call him an impostor.

IONE
We can give him a name. Endymion will do.

GLAUCUS
What god is he?

IONE
God of the moon.

GLAUCUS
Endymion, god of the moon. Well, I'll invite him.—Good sir—I mean, good …. Ione, how shall I address him?

IONE
Address him by his name.

GLAUCUS
Endymion, will your godship be pleased so far to favour my humble abode as to take up your quarters there for the night.

[**SARMION** passes his hand through **IONE'S** hair.

GLAUCUS [Aside]
Thus do the gods turn the insolence of men into courtesy. He seems smitten with

IONE

Suppose, now, my daughter were to marry a god: she would become a goddess; and I, the father of a goddess and the father-in-law of a god, would, perforce, be made a god also—a minor god. I would have been contented to be a baronet; in my dreams I have sometimes beheld myself a lord; but to be a god!—Ha! you are getting on together. I wonder, now, Endymion, for what you were made dumb. Do you know the dumby alphabet? No; well; you can write it down when we go home. Ione, I want to speak to you.

[**GLAUCUS** and **IONE** talk apart.

GLAUCUS

Would you like your father to be a god,—a minor god?

IONE

No.

GLAUCUS

But I would develop godlike qualities, of which the chief is tolerance. I begin to feel more dignified and wiser already. Then, as these qualities, by friction with other gods, and a rational indulgence in ambrosia and nectar, become brighter and solider, my minority may end, and they may give me a seat at Jove's table on Olympus, Ione, think; a little intrigue has brought about a greater matter than a divorce: Juno must be old! her successor—you do not listen: give your eyes to him and your ears to me.

IONE

I will. You were saying that you would like to be a god.

GLAUCUS

After all, I am a well-made man; and Endymion looks no more.

IONE

But he is disguised.

GLAUCUS

It may be that I am disguised too.

IONE

I doubt it: no god could be disguised so completely as not to know his own identity.

GLAUCUS

Still, here is a god punished with dumbness: Jupiter may have punished me with oblivion of a brilliant past.

IONE

What god could you possibly be?

GLAUCUS

Probably just a god. Doubtless there are gods of nothing in particular, merely decorative.

IONE
Doubtless.

GLAUCUS
Well, I would rather be that than no god at all.

IONE
I fear it.

GLAUCUS
Endymion, you must tell me in writing when we go home, if one of the chief minor gods was punished some fifty years ago by the loss of all knowledge of his own identity.

IONE
Father, he does not know a word you say:
He understands no language I can speak—
[Aside]
Except that of my eyes. If I can read
The fire of his they tell me priceless tales.

[Enter **SILENUS**, **SATYRS**, and **BACCHANTES**.

SILENUS
Ha! Ariadne!—Theseus, not yet fled!
Or who are you? But you are Ariadne.

[He is about to take her hand when **SARMION** interferes.

Bacchantes, bind him!

[After a short struggle **SARMION** is bound.

GLAUCUS
I declare! Take care what you are about, my good women; and you, old man, conduct yourself more respectfully in the presence of immortals. This is Endymion, and I am a nameless god.

SILENUS
Nameless and noteless, you! Endymion, this?
Never! I saw Endymion long ago
Before the stars were tarnished: with his crook
Sloped in his hand he wandered down a hill;
The night shone round him: this youth is not he.
Men are not made so now, though this is one
Who may remind me of the elder time.
But you, most lovely lady, seem to me
The very image of the golden age.

GLAUCUS
My daughter!

SILENUS
She is Ariadne now,
For I am Bacchus.
Fill my cup again;
If I cease drinking I grow melancholy.

[A **BACCHANTE** fills his cup and he drinks.

GLAUCUS
Pardon, most potent god!

[Enter **SCARAMOUCH, HARLEQUIN,** and **COLUMBINE**.

SILENUS
Ha! Harlequin!

SCARAMOUCH
Is that Bacchus?

HARLEQUIN
Yes.

SCARAMOUCH
Capital!—How d'ye do? how d'ye do?

SILENUS
What irrepressible person is this?

HARLEQUIN
Scaramouch.

SILENUS
I do not know the name.

SCARAMOUCH
Lamps and limpets, no! It is not in Lempriare, but it is a good name.

SILENUS
It is well you think so. What are you?

SCARAMOUCH
I am the gentleman Harlequin told you of—he who has the honour to be your majesty's most obedient
servant and impresario.

SILENUS

The showman! Well, I suppose there must be showmen.

SCARAMOUCH
Shawms and psalteries, I should think so! I can demonstrate to you that there is nothing pays but showmanship.

GLAUCUS [Aside]
This is a wise fellow.

SILENUS
You shall demonstrate nothing to me; but get us all on board your vessel as soon as possible.

SCARAMOUCH
As practical as a man! I thought all you gods were a kind of moon-struck, plaster-of-Paris, posturing, and, to say the truth, frequently indecent parcel of patriarchs. It shall appear in your advertisement, sir, 'As practical as a man.' May I be dipped in wax if it don't. The terms, sir: do you accept the offer Harlequin made?

SILENUS
You must be the son of a puppet.

SCARAMOUCH
Puppies and patchwork, why?

SILENUS
From your habit of unexpected, disjointed, and inept gesticulation, which has its exact counterpart in your pattering speeches and preposterous preludes.

SCARAMOUCH
What am I to do? The world is old; it has been satiated with originality, and in its dotage cries bitterly for entertainment. A public man must therefore be extravagant in order to distinguish himself. My felicitous alliteration and prompt non-blasphemous oaths constitute my note, which is the literary term for trade-mark—a species of catch-word, in fact. Sweetness and light! do you understand me?

SILENUS
Showman and sharper, you speak shrewdly, and I accept your terms. Come, where are your boats?

SCARAMOUCH
Oakum and orchids, there is only one!

SILENUS
One! you need a fleet.

SCARAMOUCH
Break me and splice me, if I understand!

SILENUS
How else will you ship the company before morning?

SCARAMOUCH
Company!—Harlequin, explain.

HARLEQUIN
It is true I only bargained for Bacchus, but he seems to think I meant the whole crowd.

SILENUS
All, or none.

SCARAMOUCH
Never! there was a bargain. Business!—O sacred word! Now you attack me on my weak point, which is also my strong one.

[Blows a whistle. Enter **TWO SAILORS**.

With reverential firmness remove our Bacchanalian friend.

[**SILENUS** mesmerises the **SAILORS** as they advance.

Mesmers and mystogogues! none of that! Secure the god; although he nod he cannot shake the spheres.

SAILORS
Ay, ay, sir.

1st SAILOR
Our timbers are rooted.

2nd SAILOR
Our flippers are frozen to our sides.

SCARAMOUCH
Good, my men. I shall find you an engagement as supers when we go home; but this is not the stage.

SAILORS
Ay, ay, sir.

1st SAILOR
I'm in as good form as calf's-foot jelly, and as frisky as a pyramid.

2nd SAILOR
And I'm as strong as water, and stiffer a deal than grog.

SCARAMOUCH
Ha! ha! very fine indeed. Now, truss him up and away. Do you hear? stop that acting.

SAILORS

Ay, ay, sir.

1st SAILOR
Acting? I call it doing nothing.

2nd SAILOR
I can't even scratch my head.

SCARAMOUCH [Draws his sword]
Death, distinctly, if you do not leap your own height when I count three. One, two—

[**SILENUS** makes passes and they leap.

SCARAMOUCH [Sheathes his sword]
Back to thy bed, bright babe of Birmingham! Arrest the god.

[The **SAILORS** advance, but are again mesmerised by **SILENUS**.

Sea lubbers, dare you rouse me further?

SAILORS
Ay, ay, sir.

SCARAMOUCH [Draws his sword]
Homer and homicide, then die!

[**SILENUS** mesmerises **SCARAMOUCH** just as his sword pricks **1st SAILOR**.

1st Sailor
Do not prolong my agony: run me through at once: the point pricks me, sir: in or out, one or other.

SCARAMOUCH
Magic and mastodons, I can do neither! Great Bacchus, is this a trick or no?

SILENUS
That depends on you, good Scarabee. If you consent to ship all my friends, it is a trick; but if you do not, you will find it a serious matter to stand there till you rot.

SCARAMOUCH
Every mother's son and daughter of them—the whole island, anything you like. This power of yours is worth a kingdom.

[**SILENUS** releases them.

SILENUS
Embark Ariadne in the boat you have, and send back others for the rest. Tow this egg-shell shallop with you: it is precious: its workmanship is divine.

SCARAMOUCH
Ariadne!

SILENUS
Yes; that is she.

SCARAMOUCH
Shiver my timbers! this will be the greatest combination on record.

SILENUS
Columbine, attend your mistress.

COLUMBINE
Mistress Ariadne, I am to be your waiting-maid.

IONE
I am not Ariadne.

GLAUCUS [Aside to **IONE**]
You are! you must be! Don't you see this is Bacchus, and the dumb fellow an impostor. Bacchus says he's not Endymion.

IONE [Aside to **GLAUCUS**]
It was I called him Endymion. He's no impostor.

GLAUCUS [Aside to **IONE**]
Don't argue.—Great Bacchus, Ariadne is a little bashful as becomes a maiden honoured with the attention of your godship.

SILENUS
What are you?

GLAUCUS
Her father—at least I have been so for eighteen years. I begin to doubt whether she be my child or no, since your godship perceives that she is Ariadne—a fact which I recognised the moment you mentioned it; and since certain quakings have overcome my being, revealing to me that this lodgment of clay is, as it were, a long-slumbering volcano, about to waken into full and luminous godhood.

SILENUS
Know then, that she is not your child; she is a king's daughter.

GLAUCUS
Princess Ariadne, I beseech you humbly to pardon any trouble I may have given you as a father. I here formally renounce, what was never mine, all control over your royal highness. And now, Bacchus, let us sift to the bottom this mythological mystery. First of all, what god am I? Of course I know I am only a minor one in the meantime, so do not scruple to tell me, however insignificant my rank may be.

SILENUS

We will discuss it, friend, over a bottle.—Harlequin, remove Ariadne and this youth. Good people, accompany them with singing to the shore.

IONE
Adventures throng upon me.

Song.
  The boat is chafing at our long delay,
    And we must leave too soon
  The spicy sea-pinks and the inborne spray,
    The tawny sands, the moon.

  Keep us, O Thetis, in our western flight!
    Watch from thy pearly throne
  Our vessel, plunging deeper into night
    To reach a land unknown.

[**HARLEQUIN, COLUMBINE, ARIADNE, SARMION**, go out.

SCENE III.—The Same

SILENUS, SCARAMOUCH, and **GLAUCUS** sitting round a rock. **BACCHANTES** set bottles of wine and go out.

SILENUS
Taste this, good Scarab. My little godling, drink. [All drink.

SCARAMOUCH
Body and bouquet! what is this?

SILENUS
Wine, sir, crushed from grapes the sun never ripened.

GLAUCUS
Is this to be bought?

SILENUS
What! are you still buying and selling here? Come, drink again.

[**ALL** drink.

Does it not search into the dark corners and irrigate the waste places of the brain? This will make you gods, truly. And you still buy and sell below the moon?

SCARAMOUCH

The old story, sir— East and west, and north and south, Under the crescent, or under the cross, One song you hear in every mouth, "Profit and loss, profit and loss."

SILENUS
Is it so? I should have expected some change.

GLAUCUS
Where have you been not to know that the divine institution of buying and selling is as vigorous as ever?

SILENUS
I did not know it was divine, and I have been with Bacchus among the stars.

SCARAMOUCH
Roads and railways! what does he mean?

SILENUS
And is money still the cure for all the ills of life? Is it still the talisman, eh!—my brand-new demigod? And the great and glorious institution of rich and poor, good spick-and-span divinity—is the world not tired of that gift of the gods yet?

GLAUCUS
This is empty railing: there must always be rich and poor.

SILENUS
Let the rich hope so. But drink: these thoughts unnerve me.

[**ALL** drink.

SCARAMOUCH
Good Bacchus, great Bacchus, you must be careful. Such a slip in public as you made just now would ruin us.

SILENUS
What slip did I make?

SCARAMOUCH
You talked of being with Bacchus; now, you are Bacchus.

SILENUS
So I am. Well, it was a slip.

SCARAMOUCH
Tell us about the stars.

SILENUS
Aha! good Scarab, we travelled about from planet to planet, from orb to orb, and each fresh sphere grew an original wine. As pebbles to grapes, are grapes to the fruits they crush there. Damsels, Hebes all, gather and tread them, and their ankles are stained with purple all the year round: the wine-presses

and the vats are made of scented wood: the season never changes: there is no night, no death, no rich and poor.

GLAUCUS
Glorious, Bacchus, glorious! But it seems to me that we three may now fitly discuss my mythological rank.

SILENUS
We may, good codling. Let us see. There was a god some five decades ago who lost caste abominably—no, it is longer; because during the last score centuries we Bacchanalians have been out of hearing of the faintest mundane murmur, beyond cry of Olympus, conquering the realms of space, and now visit the earth solely for Ariadne's pleasure: she had a desire to see once more her bower in Naxos.

GLAUCUS
To whom might I appeal, then? Is there no register of gods?

SCARAMOUCH
None but Lempriare.

SILENUS
It matters not: if you feel confident that you are a god you must be one.

GLAUCUS
But any one might be a god at that rate.

SILENUS
Surely, surely; confidence makes gods and goddesses of the merest mortality.

SCARAMOUCH
Mars and martyrdom! I shall be a god too.

SILENUS
Do, good Scrub, do: be a god: be the god of gulls.—I have it! Drink again.

[**ALL** drink]

By-the-bye, what has your name been hitherto?

GLAUCUS
Glaucus.

SILENUS
Then, Glaucus, know that thou art not Glaucus, but my squire, Silenus.
I am right glad to see thee, old one. Thou hast been a wanderer long.

GLAUCUS
I thank thee, Bacchus.
But I have no memory of my name or character. If thou—

SILENUS

Nay, thou must not 'thee' and 'thou' me. I am thy superior, and in my familiarity and my cups so address thee, showing my pleasure in thy return. Use respectable pronouns, Silenus. I am not angry with thee: in coming to thyself thou wilt doubtless make many mistakes, which I without resentment shall promptly correct.

GLAUCUS

Ah! great Bacchus, I seem, now, to remember with what reverence I regarded your godliness: it is the first hint my consciousness supplies of my identity. Will your great highness tell me more of myself?

SILENUS

I will, Silenus. Thou art one of those whom the bulk of gods and men pity: but thou art not truly pitiable. It is certain that thou art not a respectable immortal, for thou keepest late hours, and dost allow thy company to choose itself. I hear that thou art, or would'st be, perennially drunk: thou seemest to have as many stomachs as a cow, and art as bald as a vulture; and after thy godliness thy most indubitable attribute is certainly not thy cleanliness. No; thou art not respectable, therefore art thou pitied; but thou dost not pity thyself, wherefore I love thee. I respect the unsubduable temper of thy soul, which, in the perdition of all that mortality and immortality consider barely necessary for the mere toleration of existence, still retains its diamond edge, flashing from the worn-out scabbard, keen and serviceable for offence or defence.

GLAUCUS

But, my lord Bacchus, I shall reform.

SILENUS

Never, by Styx, thou fool! I tell thee, wert thou to change one thought of thy brain, or could'st thou obliterate one dream of thy youth, or cancel an action of thy prime, thou would'st endanger the stability of the universe. Go to: if thou reformest thou losest immortality and mortality, and shalt cease to be.

GLAUCUS

With all due respect for your godship, I do not like my character.

SILENUS

Dost thou think I like mine?

GLAUCUS

But when I was Glaucus—

SILENUS

Thou wert a fool and respectable, and did'st admire thyself. Go to.

SCARAMOUCH

Gall and wormwood! what sound is that?

SILENUS

I hear no sound.

SCARAMOUCH
A sort of tinkling.

SILENUS
O Hecate! it is the silver cymbals.

SCARAMOUCH
What cymbals?

SILENUS
Listen. Glaucus
[Aside]
The old wine-skin's going to faint.

SILENUS
He comes! he comes! great Bacchus comes! My heart! Now, foolish creatures, will you see a god. But me, alas! what punishment for me? Some wine!
[Drinks]
I'll dull my sense and show no shame.

[Empties his bottle.

This wine has lost its virtue.—Do you hear? These cymbal-players all were ladies once, Matrons and maids, close-robed from head to heel: Wild panthers' skins, zoned slackly, vest them now; Their milk-white limbs like moonbeams softly glance From tree to tree: and through the night they come.

SCARAMOUCH
Would I could hear them! But I tremble.

GLAUCUS
What does all this mean?
[Rises, drunk]
Bacchus is here, and Bacchus is there, and I'm a god, and can't understand it. I have a crude suspicion that I have taken too much wine, which a man may do once or twice in his life. My opinions about drunkenness are strong, but I will keep them to myself. Suffice it to say that I have never been drunk without good reason, and I'm not drunk now. I know the difference—any man knows the difference between exhilaration and drunkenness. I'm exhilarated now; I'm not drunk. I seem to remember another man some time or other—several men, in fact, at various times—saying that they were only exhilarated. It's a common thing to say in certain circumstances: it's a platitude. I'm not drunk. Do you think I'm drunk?

SCARAMOUCH
Drams and drachmas! as drunk's a fiddler!

GLAUCUS
Liar! liar, definitely! Put me to the test. Bacchus—give me a back!

[Runs at **SILENUS**, and falls.

SILENUS

These are the satyrs playing pandean pipes, These rippling flames of sound: the muffled notes Are tabors. How the music dwindles! Hark! From some far isle it seems to reach our ears, To reach our ears and faint: the tide-mark there Is out of hearing. I should say they pass A knoll that lies between us, or the road Winds backward, and the forest is more dense.

SCARAMOUCH

They may be going back.

SILENUS

No, Bacchus comes for me.

SCARAMOUCH

Perhaps they've lost the way.

SILENUS

Ha! ha! when Bacchus loses himself in a wood Silenus will drink the sea.

SCARAMOUCH

The sound again! It is as you say: one would think it journeyed over sea. It grows and gathers, and now it travels from its own quarter: it is very near.

SILENUS

He comes in all his state: the chariot-wheels Like silent billows roll; from side to side The tigers' heads between their velvet paws, Like lilies eyed with flame, sway noiselessly, Or, poised on high, breathe odours to the moon. Taller than Ariadne by a head He stands with her upon the chariot-floor: They have been lovers since he found her here: His arm is round her neck; one loyal hand Droops on her shoulder, and the other holds A careless rein: her face lifts up to his The deep, sweet melancholy of desire; And he looks down, high mystery in his eyes— The passionate love of these sweet centuries; Unstaunched, uncloyed.

SCARAMOUCH

But, where?—where?

SILENUS

In the wood. I know how Bacchus travels. Here they come.

SCARAMOUCH

But the tigers: we shall be eaten alive.

SILENUS

My good Scrub, the tigers of Bacchus know of daintier food than such marrowless bones and savourless flesh as you and I. The best thing you can do is to stretch yourself there beside Glaucus, and pretend that you are drunk. Bacchus may be angry at those who have carried me off, and his immediate punishment might be severe: he will do nothing to one who is in the power of wine, and by the time you can be reasonably sober his ire will have gone like the beads from a goblet.

SCARAMOUCH

I would not do so for a man, but gods may be encountered by such sleights. Honestly, I have soused my brains a little. You do not lie comfortably, Glacus. Come—why, he is sound asleep! I'll make a pillow of him.

[Lies down with his head on **GLAUCUS**.

[Enter **SATYRS** and **BACCHANTES**, followed by **BACCHUS** and **ARIADNE** in a chariot drawn by tigers. They descend.

BACCHUS
Well, runagate, who are your friends?

SILENUS
My foes:
They fell at the first bottle: I have won.

SCARAMOUCH [Aside]
I could drink him out in brandy; but these planetary wines are not for this world.

BACCHUS
How often have you run away?

SILENUS
Seven times.

BACCHUS
Seven times you've risked disaster. You are old,
Feeble and foolish—

SILENUS
Oh! not foolish, Bacchus!

BACCHUS
Hare-brained at least—

ARIADNE
But chide him not, dear lord.

BACCHUS
Well, then, I will not: he is found. Be wise,
My ancient friend, and know your happiness.

[**BACCHANTES** surround **SILENUS** and bind him with ivy.

SCARAMOUCHE [Aside]
These are gentle divinities.

ARIADNE

Here, by this sea, I waked, how long ago!
Here, by this sea, you found me.

BACCHUS

Would you be
My bride again?

ARIADNE

O no! each day, each hour
I am your bride; and as the days and years
Gather behind us, every happiness—
And that is every minute of my life—
Doubles the joy of that which went before:
And yet the past is as a galaxy
Wherein no star excels the radiant throng.

BACCHUS

Not that fair hour when first you loved me?

ARIADNE

No:
I have no memory. I am striving now
To summon up the time when here you came,
And made me an immortal and your bride.
I might as well compel my thoughts to search
For some unnoted dream that I forgot
The moment after I had told you, love,
New wakened from the sleep I dreamed it in.

BACCHUS

But memory goes afoot—invalid here:
Love has a high-commanding minister,
Imagination; and it serves alone
Beings who yield their moods and bow their minds
To its obedient masterdom: stout thought,
That trudges, blind and lame, the dusty way,
And memory, that casts its broken net
In Lethe's waves, keep not among your train—
Fit servants these for mortals.

ARIADNE

So I do—
I banish them: but still there clings to me
Something of earth.

BACCHUS

I love you best for that.

A goddess born is tame, secure of heaven,
And there is nothing to endow her with;
But you derive divinity from me,
Yet keep the passionate heart that mortals have.—
Now, I am at the morn I found you here:
Come, Ariadne, leap into the past.

ARIADNE
I cannot.

BACCHUS
See, the flying traitor's sail!

ARIADNE
No, no! This night—this hour is in my blood.
The brine, the sea-pinks, and the soaring moon
Seem thoughts of mine which now I body forth;
And these, and all the beauties of the world
Breathe of my love for you.

BACCHUS
I found you here
With crimson cheeks and nostrils wide, asleep;
Your hair dishevelled, and your mantle torn.

ARIADNE
No, no!
You cannot drive me back. I see, indeed,
A picture of our meeting; but not mine.
My fancy like a wayward messenger
Despatched to gather roses, on its wings
Bearing their scent, flies empty-handed home.

BACCHUS
What picture, Ariadne?

ARIADNE
That we saw
In Athens, when we last alighted there.
Do you remember how it made us smile
Until we felt that love had painted it;
And then we found it true and beautiful?

BACCHUS
Yes: and the poet.

ARIADNE
Oh! some mortals still

Love us, and deem us worthy of a song.
But for the subject of their art, I vow
They needs must know it better than myself
Who am the heroine: their feigning hangs
A veil before my fancy.—Come away:
Back where the water gurgles through the fern,
Dewing the feathery fronds, and hyacinths
Spread like a purple smoke far up the bank.

[Steps into the chariot.

[Enter **HARLEQUIN** and **COLUMBINE**. **SCARAMOUCH** rises.

HARLEQUIN
Bacchus!

[Is running out.

BACCHUS
Stay.

HARLEQUIN
Pardon, great Bacchus!

SCARAMOUCH
Pardon!

BACCHUS
What men are you, infesters of this isle?

SCARAMOUCH
From England come we, Bacchus—England. Ha! Know you not England, land of shams and shows?

BACCHUS
Is patriotism dead in England, then,
That travellers thus traduce their native land?
What make you here?

SCARAMOUCH
We came to hire you, sir:
I am a showman: but we took instead
Silenus here, who, pardon me, agrees
More closely with the popular idea
Of what you're like than you yourself do. Now,
What must I do? I most distinctly see
That you would be a more attractive show;
But I have made a contract with Silenus.
Then, here's the Ariadne I suppose,

And I have just returned from shipping one!
What's to be done? Stalactites, storms, and strums,
Will you come, too? Name your own price: look here:
You'll be yourself; Silenus himself, too;
And Ariadne will be Ariadne.
For her I've shipped—why, ladies have their starts,
Their turns, their maggots, and their fantasies,
Their hypochondrias, their aches, their pains,
Their dreams by day and night, their whims, their nothings;
And should her ladyship lie in the clutch,
The grip, the throes, or, to be more precise,
The mood, or mode, or manner of a qualm,
The madam I have shipped could take her place,
And be her under-study as it were.
Yea, by the very doom of destiny,
I have a substitute for you, my lord—
Endymion, they call him—in the ship!
So, Bacchus, if it happened, as it might—
And who has better reason?—that you sipped,
Or tippled, or indulged, or—Heaven forgive me!

[Falls on his knees.

Take off your eyes: they scorch me through and through!

BACCHUS [To **HARLEQUIN**]
You, with the wooden sword, I know your trade:
You shall do feats with that untempered blade.
[To **ARIADNE**]
Should you not like to see these substitutes?

ARIADNE
Rarely.

BACCHUS [To **HARLEQUIN**]
Strike, knave; and deeper than the roots
Of aged oaks, as deep as is the sea,
Wide as the Aegean, and as Olympus high,
Your striking shall be felt. Come nearer me;
Now strike, until your sword in splinters fly.

[**HARLEQUIN** strikes the earth with his sword.

SCENE IV.—Transformation from the Sea-shore to the Bower of Ariadne

Song.

Through the air, through the air,
We are borne; from our hair
A spicy odour is shaken:
We sing as we sail;
The strong trees quail,
And the dreaming doves awaken.
The pale screech-owl
That, cheek by jowl,
Goes ravening with night,
Thinks day has come,
And hurries home
Half-starved, to shun the light.
An eagle above us screams;
But a star blows a silver horn,
And a faint far echo floats
From the depths of the lakes, and the streams
Warble the shadowy notes.
A young lark thinks it morn,
And sings through our flying crowd,
That seems to his eager soul
Like a low-hung dawning cloud.
The bells of midnight toll;
The night-flowers tell the hour;
And the stately planets roll,
As we fly to our lady's bower.

SCENE V.—The Bower of Ariadne

Enter **BACCHUS** and **ARIADNE**, **SARMION** and **IONE**, **HARLEQUIN** and **COLUMBINE**, **GLAUCUS**, **SCARAMOUCH**, **SATYRS**, and **BACCHANTES**.

Song.
Here are brackens, green and gold,
Fit for plumes of Titans old;
And we see them by the light
That immortals shed at night:
Bosky rooms where to and fro
Shadowy dryads come and go;
Bubbling springs where naiads peep,
Mossy couches where they sleep.
Here beneath this tree-topped hill
Pan oft comes to pipe his fill,
Making all the valley ring;
Here the Muses sometimes sing:
And here upon this midnight hour
We visit Ariadne's bower.

ARIADNE [To **SARMION**]
Who may you be?

IONE
He cannot speak.

ARIADNE
Not speak!

BACCHUS
Silenus knows a remedy for that.

SILENUS
None better.

[Gives **SARMION** wine in a goblet.

This would loosen dead men's tongues.

SARMION
My name is Sarmion. Whence I come I know not:
I know I live; and now I have command
Of speech and of my thoughts, thanks to this wine.
I first remember being on the sea:
My shallop leapt from wave to wave: I thought
For ever to go sailing through the night:
My molten life welled from my heart and streamed
In murmuring flame through all its channels, fanned
By cooling winds: I watched the wanton waves
That melted in each other till I slept.
When I awoke the moon shone overhead,
And made along the sea a path of light,
Wherein I sailed: the beauty of it all
Blanched me with rapture; but before I knew
My shallop grounded, and I sprang on shore.
I looked about me for a silver stair
To mount up to the moon, and seeing none
Began to be dismayed, when suddenly
I came upon this lady, whom I love.
[To **IONE**]
Lady, I love you. How I longed to say
"I love you!"—We were carried to a ship,
And thence arrived here borne upon a cloud.

BACCHUS
I know you now, and what and whence you are.
I think this lady loves you in return: ask her and see.

[**SARMION** and **IONE** talk apart.

[To **SCARAMOUCH**]
So, you are he would make of me a show.

SCARAMOUCH
It is my vocation. It may be an inferior calling, but there are worse. It is not so honourable as being a god, doubtless, but it is a decent kind of beggary.

BACCHUS
I understand you have been prosperous.

SCARAMOUCH
On the whole I have. I am not yet a millionaire, but I have capital. I—don't look at me like that!

BACCHUS
Prosperity has spoiled you, sir, I see:
You need to view the world with other eyes.
Come, Harlequin, that splinter of your sword
Shall work an old-world metamorphosis.
Strike him between the shoulders.

[**HARLEQUIN** strikes **SCARAMOUCH**.

To an ape
Be changed: and in that form you shall be caught,
And pass on exhibition for a year
From John-o'-Groat's to Land's End, up and down:
Thereafter you shall be a man again.

SCARAMOUCH
Monkeys, menageries and misery! Bacchus, Bacchus, think what you do! Do I merit such a fate? Make me a toad, a rat, a cockroach! Heavens! a monkey in a cage! Straw, stench, and filth; and little boys to tickle me with sticks, and throw me nuts! A blinking bleared baboon! A chattering, gibbering, jabbering—

[**SCARAMOUCH** rushes out transformed to an ape.

BACCHUS [To **GLAUCUS**]
Come hither.

GLAUCUS [Aside]
Now shall I grow young again, and be the god I am—and yet I tremble.

BACCHUS
You look like one who thinks himself of note.

GLAUCUS

Surely, sir, surely. I am Silenus, your high godship's faithful old servant. I wish I could see myself. Have I undergone a change similar to your godship's? When I last saw you—I remember nothing since I fell asleep by the sea-shore—you were an old blown blue-bottle; now you are as I see you. Am I now a god? Have I cast my slough?

SILENUS

Oho! I have a word to say. You must know that I played Bacchus in my wanderings. This vain old coxcomb took it into his head that he must be a god, whereupon I persuaded him that he was myself, though all Olympus knows there's not much of the god about me.

GLAUCUS

What! have I been played upon like a kettledrum? Is this all a dream?

BACCHUS

Well, are you still an immortal?

GLAUCUS

No—no; I am a foolish old man.

BACCHUS

I'm glad you think so: you can now go home.

GLAUCUS

My daughter, sir?

BACCHUS

Is safe. Farewell.

[**GLAUCUS** goes out.

[To **HARLEQUIN** and **COLUMBINE**]
Come here.

HARLEQUIN and **COLUMBINE**

Mercy! mercy!

BACCHUS

Will you return, or will you follow me?

HARLEQUIN and **COLUMBINE**

O send us back!

BACCHUS

A wretched choice: but go.

[**HARLEQUIN** and **COLUMBINE** go out.

Sarmion, what says the lady to your love?

SARMION
O words of wonder, of enchantment—sweet,
And yet so strong, so tender and so bold,
That any ears save mine would miss the sense,
The savour, the aroma that they bear.

ARIADNE
You love him, then?

IONE
Yes.

ARIADNE
And you told him so?

IONE
I did.

ARIADNE
What wondrous language could you use
That he should be so frenzied?

IONE
I but spoke
The language of my heart.

BACCHUS
Well answered, girl.—
Our time is brief, for we have far to go
Before this side of earth can roll again
Out of its shadow. Listen, lovers.

SILENUS
Peace.

BACCHUS
Sarmion, you are descended from a race
Inhabiting a star above the moon.
Spirits they are, and by a subtle thought
Spirits are born to them. Those sultry clouds
That surge in slumbrous ranks like golden waves,
Or on the skyline of the earth build up,
Agleam with topaz and with sardonyx,
Towards evening, high pavilions and towers,
That change to lofty crests and gorges deep
The fancy cannot fathom, are more dense,

More gross than the ethereal continents
Of yonder orb, washed by a sinuous sea
Guiltless of storm, thinner and lovelier
Than the divided azure. In a dream
You had a vision of an earthly maid;
And, still asleep, your life, on fire for her,
Shaped to itself the body that you have—
The first to be incarnate of your race:
And then the secret limbec of your love
Distilled the wing'd and airy boat of pearl
That bore you to the earth. Here you awoke,
The past, forgot—the present, wonder all.

ARIADNE
But shall we visit soon this star of his?

BACCHUS
Sometime we shall.—Sarmion, this choice is yours:
Either to give Ione up, and be
Again a free thought in your natal sphere,
Whose whole dimensions, tense and rare, are pierced
By dwellers there, and give as easy way
As summer air to swallows, as the deep
To sporting dolphins; or to have your love
And with her the imprisonment of earth,
Where spirit must be draped in mortal flesh,
Where motion's shackled, and where ways are hewn,
Where life is conscious, and where death ends all.

SARMION
I choose Ione.
What with her must come
I scarcely understand; but there can fall
No present woe so bitter as would be
Her absence from my life.

IONE
O love, think well!
Here are disease and care; I shall grow old;
And poverty may catch us in its net.

SARMION
Your voice is music, but you speak of things
Unknown to me.

IONE
Then, though my heart must break,
Return, return! This world is not for you!

A thousand daily pitfalls mesh the path
Of those who here are native: faults in friends,
Denials, tarryings, storm, and heat and cold,
Things loathsome, incomplete; falsehood, and wrath:
O I am ill at saying what I mean!
Think; if these pitiful disquietings
Have power to kill the joy in us, who come
Of blood that never beat in other veins
Than those of men and women, still abused
By buffetings of chance on every side,
What misery, what terror will there be
For you, whose life has known no bolts, no bars,
No stumbling-blocks, no weariness, no care!
And, chief of all, when you begin to find,
How weak, how foolish, and how fond I am!

SARMION
Have you to suffer daily miseries?
Then here I stay. Gaunt wretchedness, advance:
If I may have this maiden for my mate,
No sting, no stroke of yours can make me quail;
And while I live I cannot be so bruised
But some sound part of me shall have the strength
To bear the blows intended for my love.

IONE
Now, God forbid! 'Tis I shall be your shield.

ARIADNE
Come here and kiss me.

[**ARIADNE** embraces Ione.

BACCHUS
This is well, indeed.—
We must, ere dawn, away to India:
You two shall be transported through the air
To Glaucus' house.

IONE
How far are we from home?

BACCHUS
Three miles, I think.

IONE
O, pray you, let us walk!
Sarmion, three miles together through the wood

Shimmering with moonlight, full of smothered sound,
And ghostly shadow, and the mingled scent
Of flowers and spices, and the cooling earth!
It is a very lifetime of delight!

BACCHUS
Good-night then, and farewell.

ARIADNE
Farewell.

IONE
Farewell.

SARMION
All happiness go with you into Ind.

[**SARMION** and **IONE** go out.

ARIADNE
This star, my love—I burn to see this star.

BACCHUS
You shall upon your birthday.

ARIADNE
Two weeks hence,
As mortals count! Well, I can wait.

BACCHUS
Lead on.

John Davidson – A Short Biography

John Davidson was born at Barrhead, East Renfrewshire on 11th April 1857, the son of Alexander Davidson, an Evangelical Union minister and Helen née Crocket of Elgin.

In 1862 the family moved to Greenock and Davidson began his education at Highlanders' Academy. From there he began his career, aged a mere 13, at the chemical laboratory of Walker's Sugarhouse refinery. A year later he returned to Highlander's, this time as a pupil teacher.

During his later employment at the Public Analysts' Office, 1870–71 he developed a keen interest in science which later became an important characteristic of his poetry. He returned once again to the Highlander's Academy, this time for four years, in 1872, again as a pupil teacher. In 1876 he spent a year at Edinburgh University before his first scholastic employment at Alexander's Charity, Glasgow which led to short periods of employment at various other schools over the following half a dozen years.

This led to a stint at Morrison's Academy in Crieff (1885–88), and in a private school at Greenock (1888–89).

In 1885 Davidson married Margaret McArthur and the marriage produced two children, Alexander (born in 1887) and Menzies (born in 1889).

Davidson's first published work was 'Bruce, A Chronicle Play', written in the Elizabethan style, and published by a local Glasgow imprint in 1886. Four other plays quickly followed; 'Smith, A Tragic Farce' (1888), 'An Unhistorical Pastoral' (1889), 'A Romantic Farce' (1889), and then the somewhat brilliant pantomime 'Scaramouch in Naxos' (1889).

By now he was very much immersed in literature and, in 1889, he ventured to London where he frequented the famous Fleet Street pub 'Ye Olde Cheshire Cheese' and joined the 'Rhymers' Club', a poets group that was based there.

Davidson was a prolific and hard-working writer. As well as his plays he wrote for the Speaker, the Glasgow Herald, and several other papers. He also wrote and had published several novels and tales, with perhaps the best being 'Perfervid' (1890).

With his reputation gradually providing an income he was also able to explore his true medium; Verse. 'In a Music Hall and Other Poems' (1891) together with 'Fleet Street Eclogues' (1893) were ample proof that he possessed a quite rare, genuine and distinctive poetic gift. Praise came from his peers including George Gissing and WB Yeats who wrote that it was: 'An example of a new writer seeking out new subject matter, new emotions'.

Davidson now turned further and further towards verse. In 1894 he published his most popular volume, 'Ballads and Songs' (1894), and this was followed by a further 'Fleet Street Eclogues' (Second Series) (1896) and by 'New Ballads' (1897) and 'The Last Ballad' (1899).

Davidson was a prolific writer. Besides the works cited, he wrote many other works including, 'The Wonderful Mission of Earl Lavender' (1895), a novel which extends his literary canon to flagellation erotica. He also contributed an introduction to Shakespeare's Sonnets (Renaissance edition, 1908), which, like his various prefaces and essays, shows him to be a subtle literary critic.

As the new century dawned Davidson was hard at work on a series of 'Testaments', in which he gave definite expression to his philosophy and these were published over a seven year period; 'The Testament of a Vivisector' (1901), 'The Testament of a Man Forbid' (1901), 'The Testament of an Empire Builder' (1902), and 'The Testament of John Davidson' (1908).

Though he played down any thought of himself as a philosopher, he expounded an original philosophy which was at once materialistic and aristocratic.

His later verse, which is often fine rhetoric rather than poetry, expressed his belief which is summed up in the last words that he wrote, "Men are the universe become conscious; the simplest man should consider himself too great to be called after any name." Davidson professed to reject all existing philosophies, including that of Nietzsche, as inadequate. The poet planned to expand and expound on his revolutionary creed in a trilogy entitled 'God and Mammon'. Only two plays, however, were written, 'The Triumph of Mammon' (1907) and 'Mammon and his Message' (1908).

In addition to his own work Davidson was a noted translator of other works which included Montesquieu's 'Lettres Persanes' (1892), François Coppée's 'Pour la Couronne' in 1896 and Victor Hugo's 'Ruy Blas' in 1904, the former being produced as, 'For the Crown', at the Lyceum Theatre in 1896, the latter as 'A Queen's Romance' at the Imperial Theatre.

Frank Harris, a member of the Rhymers' Club and himself a writer of erotic literature described him in 1889 as: "... a little below middle height, but strongly built with square shoulders and remarkably fine face and head; the features were almost classically regular, the eyes dark brown and large, the forehead high, the hair and moustache black. His manners were perfectly frank and natural; he met everyone in the same unaffected kindly human way; I never saw a trace in him of snobbishness or incivility. Possibly a great man, I said to myself, certainly a man of genius, for simplicity of manner alone is in England almost a proof of extraordinary endowment."

In 1906 he was awarded a civil list pension of £100 per annum and George Bernard Shaw did what he could to help him financially. However other issues were also circling besides poverty. Ill-health, and his declining intellectual powers, amplified by the onset of cancer, caused profound hopelessness and clinical depression.

Late in 1908, Davidson left London to live in Penzance in Cornwall. On 23rd March 1909, he left his house and was not seen again. There seemed no sound reason not to believe that he had done so with the intention of drowning himself. On an examination of his office a new manuscript was found. It was a poetry book; 'Fleet Street Poems', with a letter bleakly stating confirming, "This will be my last book."

Indeed in his philosophic book 'The Testament of John Davidson', published the year before his death, he anticipates this fate:

"None should outlive his power. . . . Who kills
Himself subdues the conqueror of kings;
Exempt from death is he who takes his life;
My time has come."

Davidson's body was not discovered until 18th September in Mount's cave by some fishermen. In accordance with his will it was now buried at sea. Strangely it seemed Davidson's wish that none of his unpublished works, nor any biography be published and "no word except of my writing is ever to appear in any book of mine as long as the copyright endures."

Davidson's poetry was a key early influence on important Modernist poets, in particular, his compatriot Hugh MacDiarmid, Wallace Stevens and T.S. Eliot.

John Davidson – A Concise Bibliography

The North Wall (1885)
Diabolus Amans (1885) Verse drama

Bruce (1886) A drama in five acts
Smith (1888) A tragedy
An Unhistorical Pastoral, A Romantic Farce (1889)
Scaramouch in Naxos (1889)
Perfervid: The Career of Ninian Jamieson (1890) with 23 Original Illustrations by Harry Furniss
The Great Men, And a Practical Novelist (1891) Illustrated by E. J. Ellis.
In a Music Hall, and other Poems (1891)
Laura Ruthven's Widowhood (with C. J. Wills) (1892)
Fleet Street Eclogues (1893)
The Knight of the Maypole, (1903)
Sentences and Paragraphs (1893)
Ballads and Songs (1894)
Baptist Lake (1894)
A Random Itinerary (1894)
A Full and True Account of the Wonderful Mission of Earl Lavender (1895)
St. George's Day (1895)
Fleet Street Eclogues (Second Series) (1896)
Miss Armstrong's and Other Circumstances (1896)
The Pilgrimage of Strongsoul and Other Stories (1896)
New Ballads (1897)
Godfrida, a play (1898)
The Last Ballad (1899)
Self's the Man, A tragi-comedy (1901)
The Testament of a Man Forbid (1901)
The Testament of a Vivisector (1901)
The Testament of an Empire Builder (1902)
A Rosary (1903)
The Knight of the Maypole: A Comedy in Four Acts (1903)
The Testament of a Prime Minister (1904)
The Ballad of a Nun (1905)
The Theatrocrat: A Tragic Play of Church and State (1905)
Holiday and other poems, with a note on poetry (1906)
The Triumph of Mammon (1907)
Mammon and His Message (1908)
The Testament of John Davidson (1908)
Fleet Street and other Poems (1909)

He was also a contributor to 'The Yellow Book' periodical

As Translator

Montesquieu's Lettres Persanes (Persian Letters) (1892)
François Coppée's Pour la couronne (For the Crown) (1896)
Victor Hugo's Ruy Blas (A Queen's Romance) (1904)

www.ingramcontent.com/pod-product-compliance
Lightning Source LLC
Chambersburg PA
CBHW021945040426
42448CB00008B/1253